Mel Bay Presents

Folk Songs of America and the British Isles

for Easy to Intermediate Guitar Ensemble

**Transcribed and Arranged by
Joseph Mayes, Glenn Caluda and Manley Mallard**

Score

1 2 3 4 5 6 7 8 9 0

© 2004 BY MEL BAY PUBLICATIONS, INC., PACIFIC, MO 63069.
ALL RIGHTS RESERVED. INTERNATIONAL COPYRIGHT SECURED. B.M.I. MADE AND PRINTED IN U.S.A.
No part of this publication may be reproduced in whole or in part, or stored in a retrieval system, or transmitted in any form
or by any means, electronic, mechanical, photocopy, recording, or otherwise, without written permission of the publisher.

Visit us on the Web at www.melbay.com — E-mail us at email@melbay.com

Table of Contents

1 All Through the Night p.6

2. The Ash Grove p.9

3. Annie Laurie p.14

4. Barbara Allen p.21

5. Geordie p.24

6. Drink to Me Only With Thine Eyes p.27

7. The Last Rose of Summer p.31

8. My Bonnie Lies Over the Ocean p.34

9. Three Ravens p.39

10. Shenandoah p.42

Introduction

The music in this small collection of folk songs from America and the British Isles have an agelessness and familiarity that combine to make them accessible and enjoyable. They are presented here arranged to be played by a quartet of guitarists of beginning to intermediate ability, but are versatile and attractive enough to be useful as duets or trios by players of more experience. This edition presents a four-part setting of each folk song followed by a variation. Only the first guitar part goes higher than the fifth fret, and then only sparingly. The arrangements can be played by different types of guitars, including classical, steel string, electric, fingerstyle, and pick style in various combinations. They can also be played by guitars in combination with other instruments. Page turns are kept to a minimum. For those directors more at home on the piano, a piano score is also included. Within the style of this music, parallel intervals (5ths' and octaves) are often desirable.

1. All Through the Night

This tune is a Welsh folk song that first appears in printed music in 1784. The words have undergone a transformation from those first associated with the tune by Amelia Opie. These had to do with "Poor Mary Ann." The "All Through the Night" lyrics were written by Harold Boulton.

2. Ash Grove

The Ash Grove was originally a Welsh harp tune called "Llwyn Onn." The words most often heard today are a longing for the singer's dear one who rests " 'neath the green turf down by the ash grove." There are, however, at least seven Welsh and sixteen English lyrics (including one quite baudy one called "The Mayor of Bayswater's Daughter"). John Gay used the tune in his Beggar's Opera (1728) with the title, "Cease your funning."

3. Annie Laurie

Believe it or not, there was an actual Annie Laurie. She was the daughter of Sir Robert Laurie, first Baronet of Maxwelton, Scotland. The first lyrics were believed to have been written by Annie's unsuccessful suitor William Douglas. The song was very popular with British troops in the Crimean War, and has been a much loved American folk song for over one hundred years.

4. Barbara Allen

On January 2, 1666, Samuel Pepys wrote about a performance of this song by the actress Mrs. Knipp. Oliver Goldsmith was moved to tears when his dairy maid sang it. Horace Greeley, in Recollections of a Busy Life, speaks of his mother singing it. In short, this song has been around for a very long time and enjoys hundreds of variants on the lyrics. The original came from Scotland at the beginning of the seventeenth century, and captured the imagination of those who heard it because of the universality of its theme: evil woman doing wrong to hapless man.

5. Geordie

The song, Geordie, has been attributed to a wonderful array of people and circumstances. What we know for sure is that it was collected by Cecil Sharp and made famous by Joan Baez. The words are essentially pleading the cause of a poacher by his lady-love (or his mother depending on the version). The haunting beauty of the music is a plaintive lament which underscores the unsuccessful plea.

6. Drink to Me Only With Thine Eyes

The words of this song came from Letters by the third century Greek poet Philostratus of Athens. It was published as translated by Ben Jonson in his 1616 <u>The Forest</u>. The music has been attributed to Mozart and also to a man named Colonel Millish.

7. Last Rose of Summer

The Last Rose of Summer's words were written by Thomas Moore over an old Irish tune called "My Lodging is on the Cold Cold Ground." Moore made a career of putting his own words to traditional Irish aires, and his twelve publications of ten songs each earned him 100 guineas for each song. These books were called Melodies, and spread across Europe and America setting the pace for "parlor-balladry" in the nineteenth century.

8. My Bonnie Lies Over the Ocean

The original Scottish folk song, My Bonnie, has been lost for over a century. In 1881 Charles E. Pratt, writing under not one but two pseudonyms - J.T. Wood and H.J. Fulmer, words and music respectively - wrote the song that we now know. It was an instant success with colleges, barbershop singers, campers, schools, and almost everyone else.

9. Three Ravens

This song is from Melismata by Thomas Ravenscroft published in 1611. Ravenscroft is also responsible for the perennial favorite Three Blind Mice. The words concern themselves with death, duty, and honor.

10. Shenandoah

This sea chantey began as a land based song along the Mississippi and Missouri Rivers. It tells of a trader who fell in love with the daughter of the indian chief Shenandoah. It became a favorite of blue-water sailors, and stayed in the folk tradition after the end of the age of sail. It was a favorite with the American Cavalry, who called it "The Wild Mizzourye".

All Through the Night

The Ash Grove

Annie Laurie

Barbara Allen

Geordie

Drink to Me Only With Thine Eyes

The Last Rose of Summer

My Bonnie Lies Over the Ocean

35

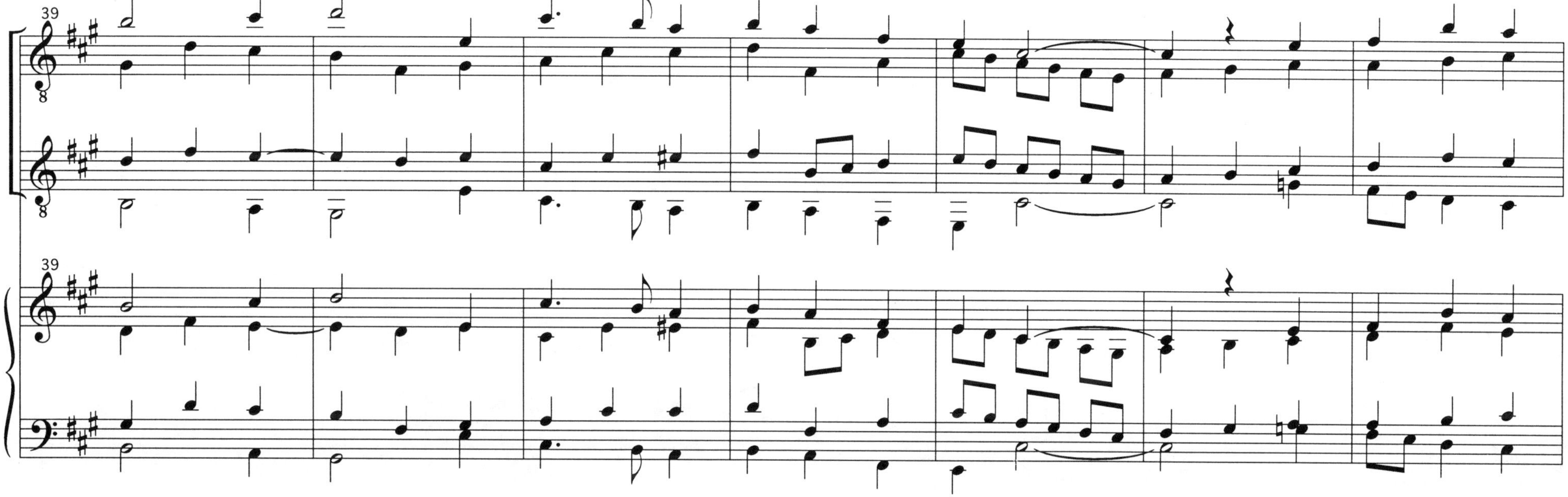
39
39

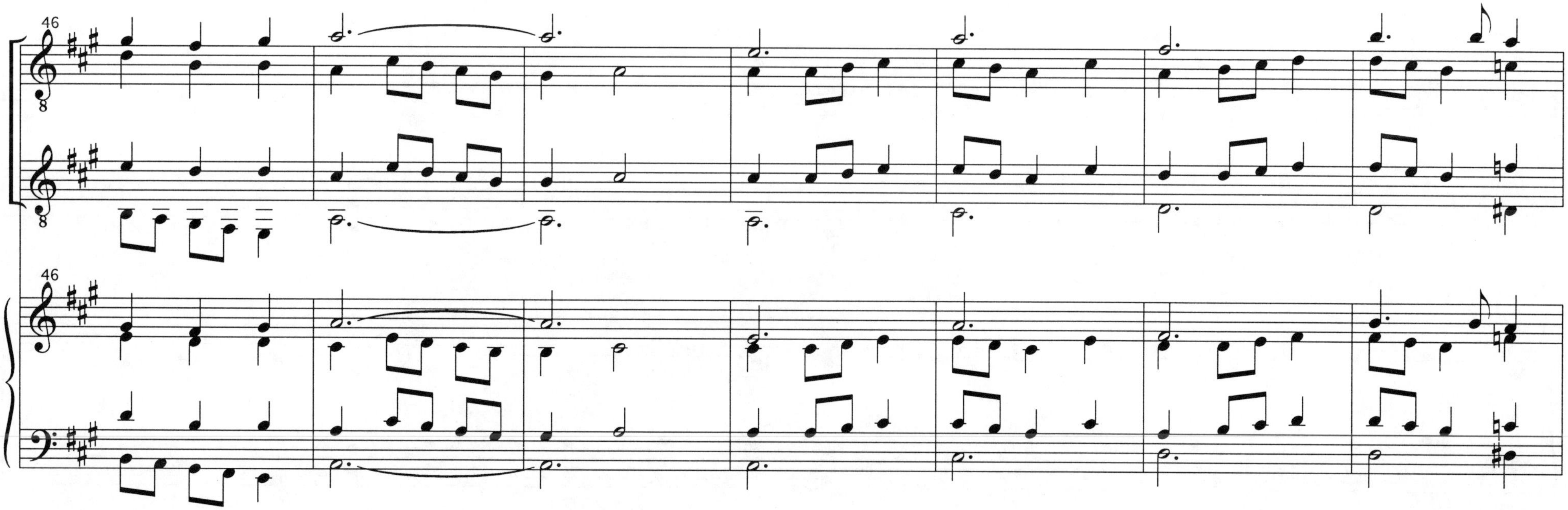
46
46

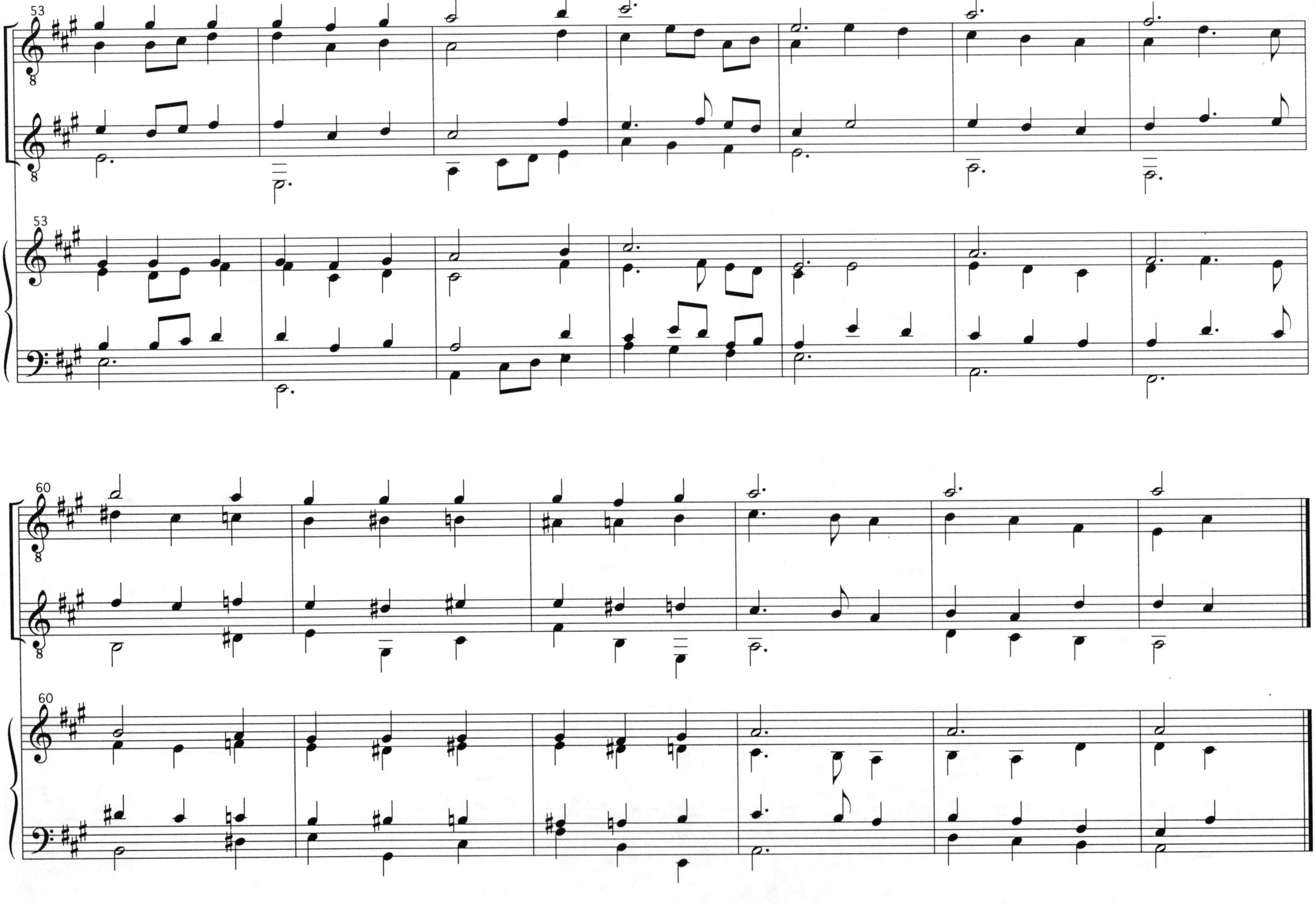
53
53
60
60

The Three Ravens

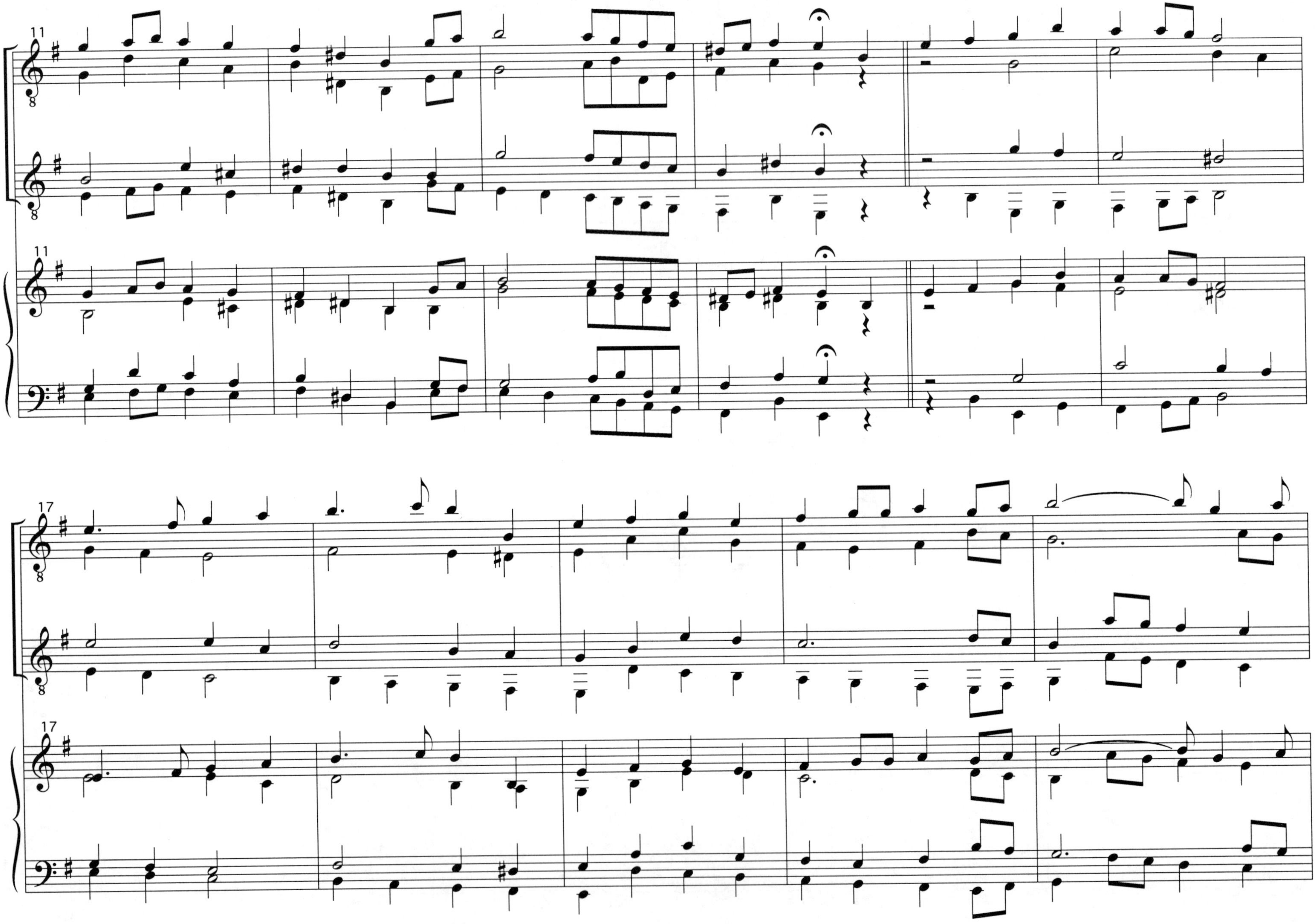
11
11
17
17

41

Shenandoah

43

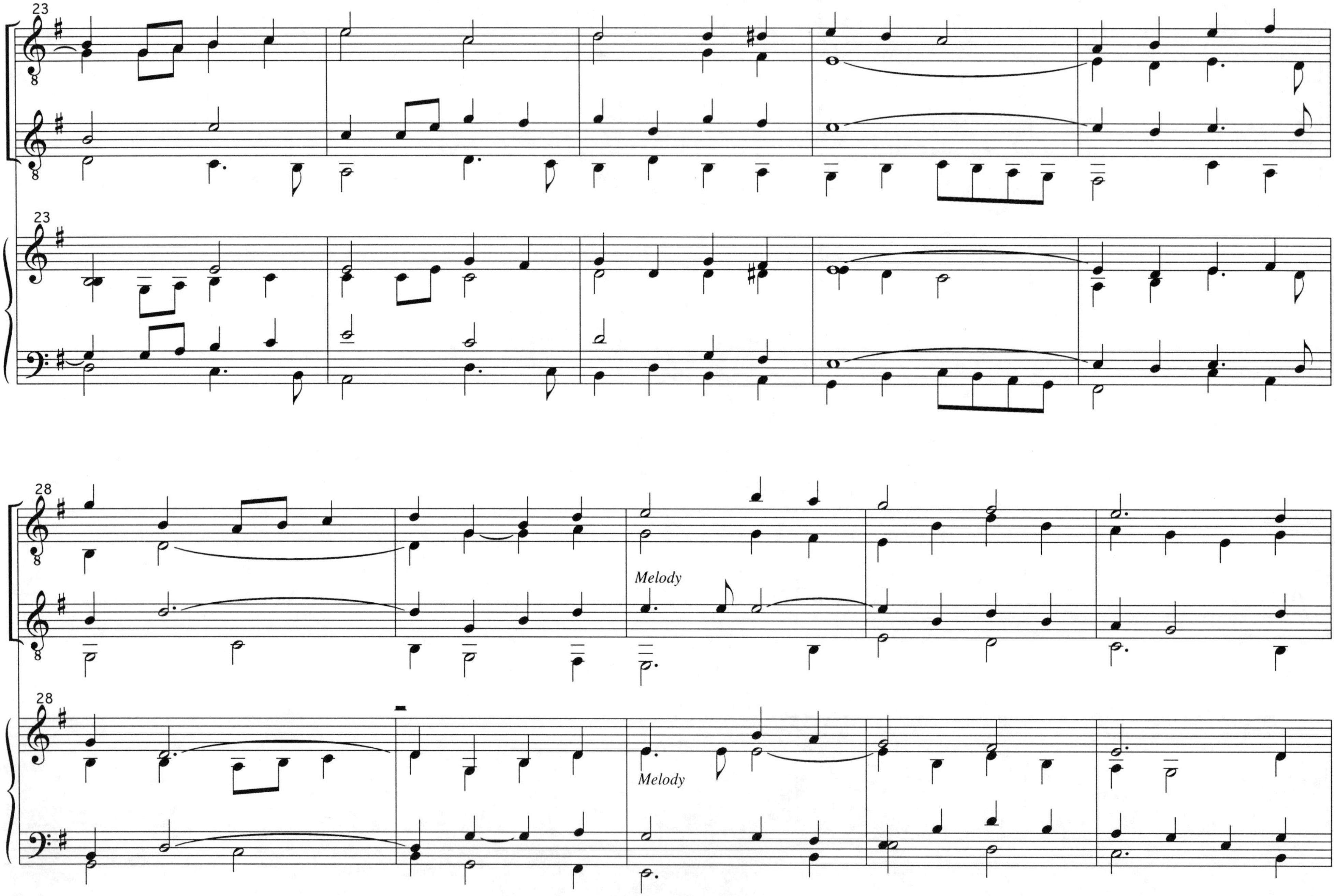
23
23
28
Melody
28
Melody

45

Joseph Mayes

Joseph Mayes was self-taught until 1963 when he began his studies with Mr. Peter Colona at the Settlement Music School in Philadelphia. In 1968, after three years in the army, Mr. Mayes was given an invitational scholarship by the government of Spain to study with the internationally-renowned concert guitarist Andres Segovia at the "Musica en Compostela" Festival in Santiago de Compostela, Spain. Since that master class, he has studied with such notable teachers as Carlos Barbosa-Lima, Glenn Caluda, José Tomas, and Oscar Ghiglia. Mayes holds degrees in guitar from Thomas Edison College of Trenton, New Jersey, and Shenandoah University of Winchester, Virginia.

Since 1972, Mr. Mayes has been on the faculty of Rowan University where he teaches guitar, lute, vihuela, and mandolin. His arrangements and transcriptions for guitar, guitar ensemble and guitar with other instruments have been published by Galvanized Music, Plucked String, Inc. and Mel Bay Publications, Inc. His recordings span the complete range of the enormous repertoire for the guitar and lute. His latest CD is a collection of salon music entitled "Parlor Gems", performed on recreations of authentic 19th Century guitars.

Mayes made his London debut at Wigmore Hall in January of 1981, and later that year his New York debut at the Carnegie Recital Hall. He has appeared on television and radio and his concertizing has taken him throughout Europe and to more than half of the fifty states.

Glenn Caluda

Glenn Caluda was born in New Orleans, Louisiana, and received a Bachelor of Music Education degree from Louisiana State University in Baton Rouge. From 1970-1973, he served as guitarist and bassist with the Soldiers' Chorus of the United States Army Field Band of Washington, DC. After military service, Mr. Caluda taught guitar at the Community College of Baltimore. He attended the University of Maryland and received a Master of Arts degree in Music Education. In 1975, he became the first full time guitar teacher at Shenandoah College and Conservatory (now Shenandoah University) in Winchester, Virginia, where he has established a classical guitar program and added new curricula. He received a Ph.D. in Music Education from Louisiana State University in 1985.

Mr. Caluda has studied guitar with the renowned guitar pedagogue Aaron Shearer as well as other fine teachers and players. He has given classes and clinics at various state and national music educators' conventions. His publications include journal articles, compositions for solo guitar, arrangements for guitar ensemble, and music for children's choir. Mr. Caluda is also an active performer as a soloist and in various ensembles.

Manley Mallard

Manley Mallard is currently on faculty at Millikin University in Decatur, Illinois where he is Coordinator of Guitar Studies and teaches classical and jazz guitar, music theory, computer notation and sequencing software and directs guitar and studio ensembles. Mr. Mallard holds degrees from Shenandoah University, Kent State and Webster University and has studied with Manuel Fraguela, Glenn Caluda, Christoph Harlan and Steve Schenkel. A talented and versatile guitarist, Mr. Mallard has performed throughout the Midwest in a variety of venues from the concert stage to night clubs. In the Spring of 1991, Mr. Mallard founded and initiated the first Mid-America Guitar Ensemble Festival, now in its thirteenth year and attracts over 150 participants. Mr. Mallard's arrangements and transcriptions are published by Guitar Chamber Music Press, Plucked String Inc. and Mel Bay Publications, Inc.